JOSEPH MIDTHUN   SAMUEL HITI

BUILDING BLOCKS OF SCIENCE

THE ENDOCRINE AND REPRODUCTIVE SYSTEMS

WORLD
BOOK

a Scott Fetzer company
Chicago

www.worldbook.com

World Book, Inc.
180 North LaSalle Street
Suite 900
Chicago, Illinois 60601
USA

For information about other World Book publications,
visit our website at www.worldbook.com
or call 1-800-WORLDBK (967-5325).
For information about sales to schools and libraries,
call 1-800-975-3250 (United States),
or 1-800-837-5365 (Canada).

Library of Congress Cataloging-in-Publication Data

The endocrine and reproductive systems.
    pages cm. -- (Building blocks of science)
    Includes index.
    Summary: "A graphic nonfiction volume that
introduces the endocrine and reproductive systems
of the human body"-- Provided by publisher.
    ISBN 978-0-7166-1844-7
    1. Endocrine glands--Juvenile literature.
2. Generative organs--Juvenile literature. 3. Human
reproduction--Juvenile literature. I. World Book, Inc.
QP187.E525 2014
612.4--dc23
                            2013025432

Building Blocks of Science
ISBN: 978-0-7166-1840-9 (set, hc.)

Printed in China by Shenzhen Donnelley
Printing Co., Ltd., Guangdong Province
3rd printing May 2016

Acknowledgments:
Created by Samuel Hiti and Joseph Midthun
Art by Samuel Hiti
Written by Joseph Midthun
Special thanks to Syril McNally

TABLE OF CONTENTS

There is a glossary on page 30. Terms defined in the glossary
are in type **that looks like this** on their first appearance.

THE ENDOCRINE SYSTEM

Your body is made up of tiny organisms called **cells.**

Like us!

Cells work together to make up **tissues** in your body.

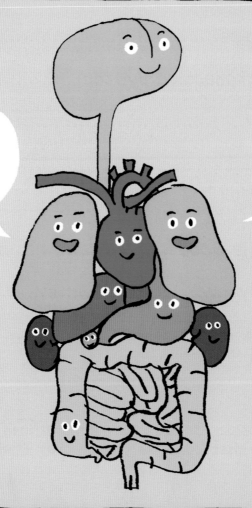

These tissues form **organs** that work together as systems inside you!

Every cell inside you has a life cycle.

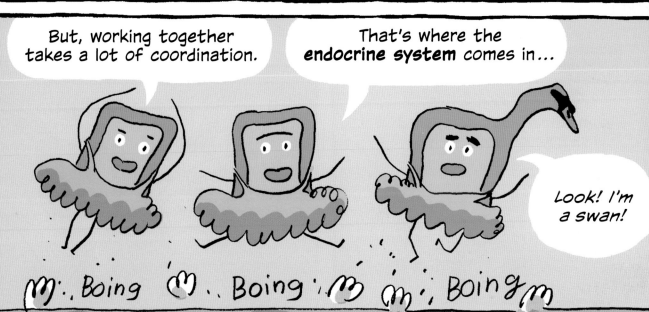

CONTROLLING CHEMICALS

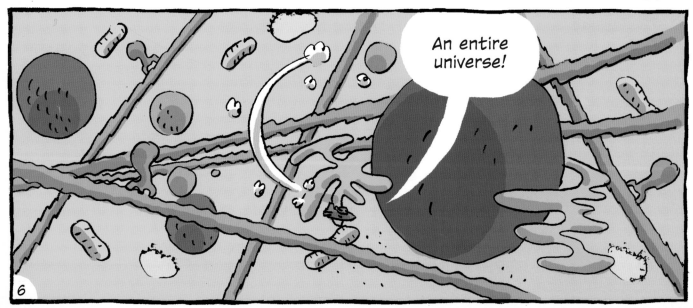

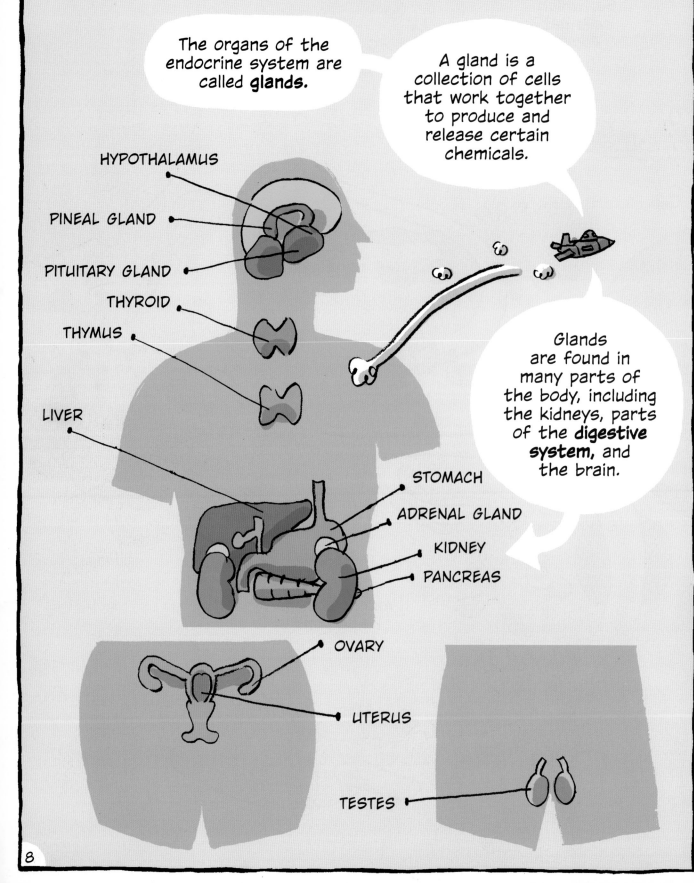

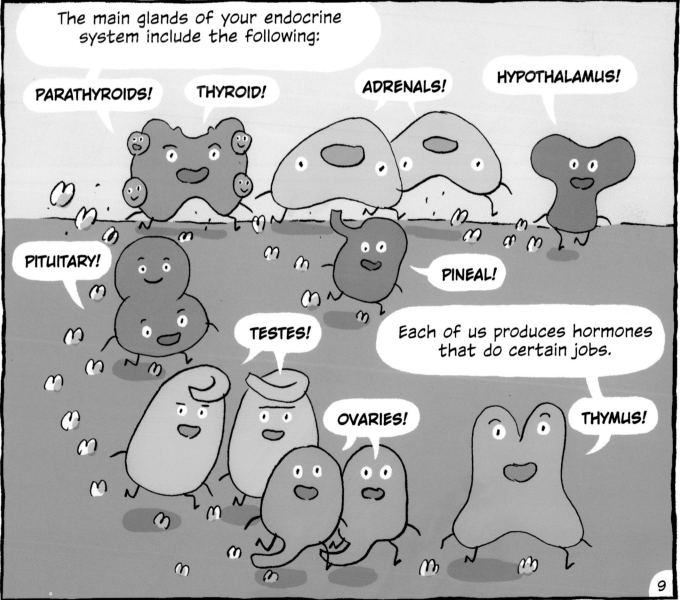

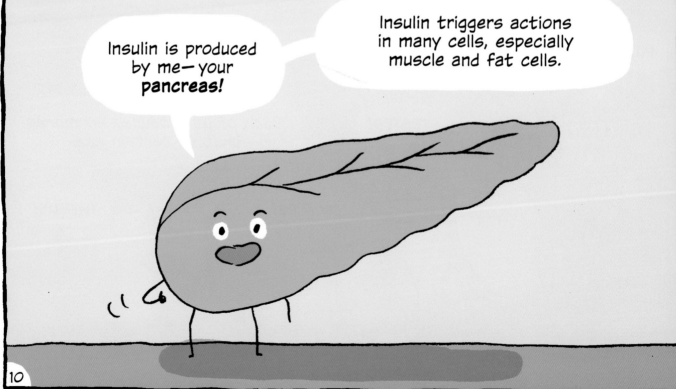

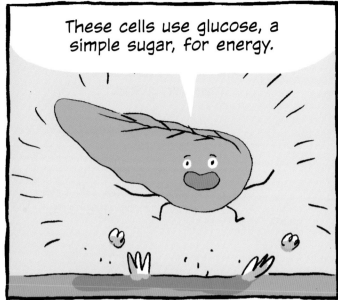

These cells use glucose, a simple sugar, for energy.

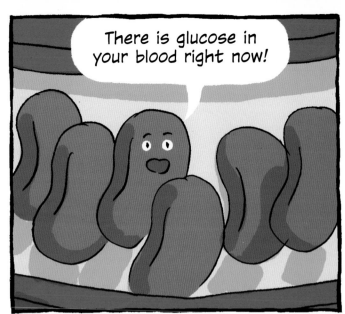

There is glucose in your blood right now!

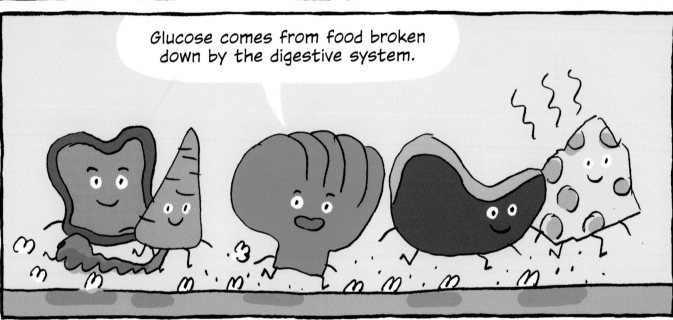

Glucose comes from food broken down by the digestive system.

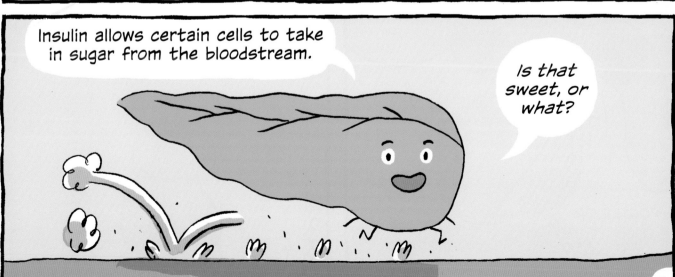

Insulin allows certain cells to take in sugar from the bloodstream.

Is that sweet, or what?

OTHER GLANDS

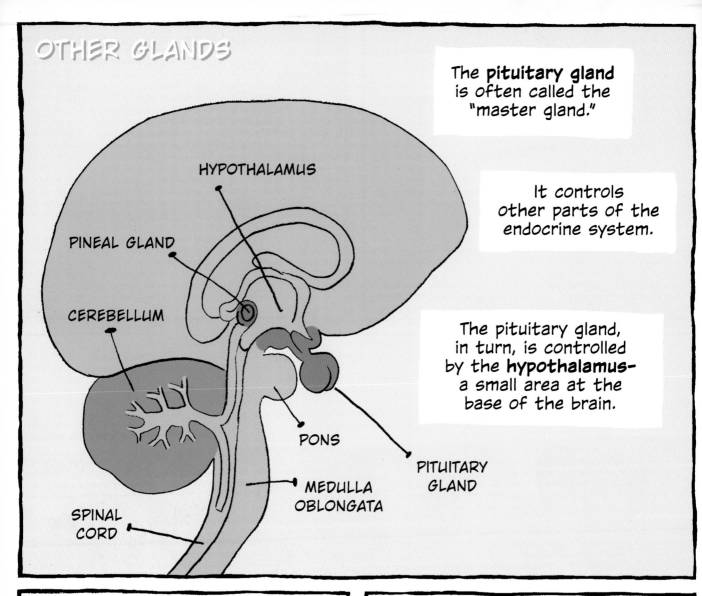

HYPOTHALAMUS

PINEAL GLAND

CEREBELLUM

PONS

MEDULLA OBLONGATA

PITUITARY GLAND

SPINAL CORD

The **pituitary gland** is often called the "master gland."

It controls other parts of the endocrine system.

The pituitary gland, in turn, is controlled by the **hypothalamus**—a small area at the base of the brain.

The pituitary gland has two **lobes.**

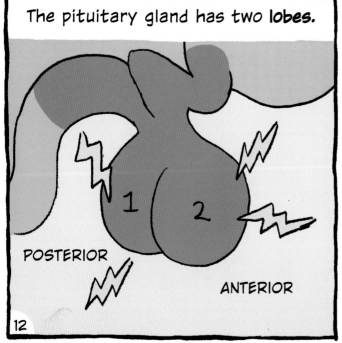

POSTERIOR

ANTERIOR

1

2

The posterior lobe receives hormones from the hypothalamus.

The anterior lobe makes and sends other hormones to parts of the body.

The pineal gland releases a hormone called melatonin.

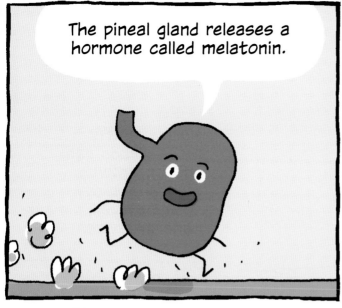

Melatonin helps you fall asleep.

Z.

Darkness stimulates the body to produce more melatonin...

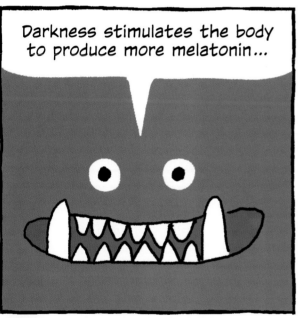

...and light blocks the production of melatonin.

click

When more melatonin is produced, you grow tired.

YAWN...

When less melatonin is produced, you start to wake up.

WHA?!

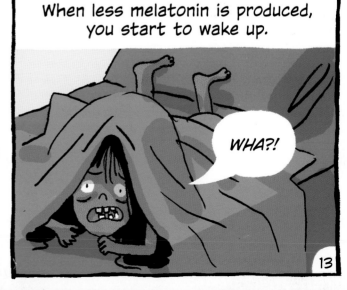

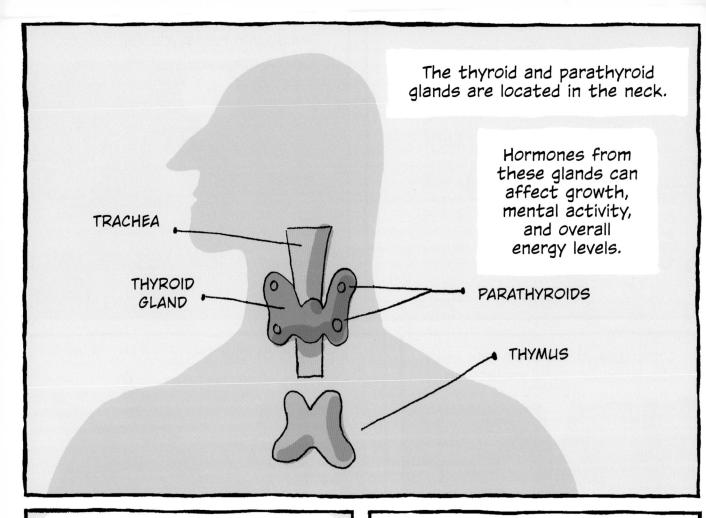

The thyroid and parathyroid glands are located in the neck.

Hormones from these glands can affect growth, mental activity, and overall energy levels.

TRACHEA

THYROID GLAND

PARATHYROIDS

THYMUS

The parathyroids regulate levels of calcium in the blood.

Your thyroid controls the rate at which your cells convert energy, among other important tasks.

Wow!

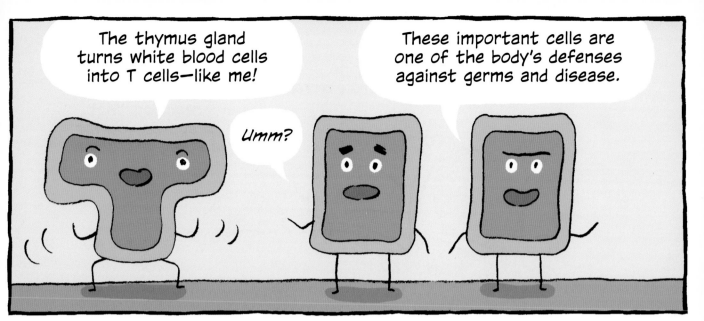

The thymus gland turns white blood cells into T cells—like me!

These important cells are one of the body's defenses against germs and disease.

Umm?

I also produce hormones that help T cells develop into maturity.

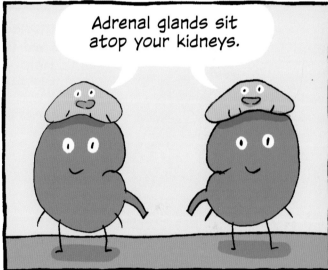

Adrenal glands sit atop your kidneys.

We produce hormones that help control how the body uses **nutrients**...

...such as sugars, starches, proteins, and fats.

15

STRESS

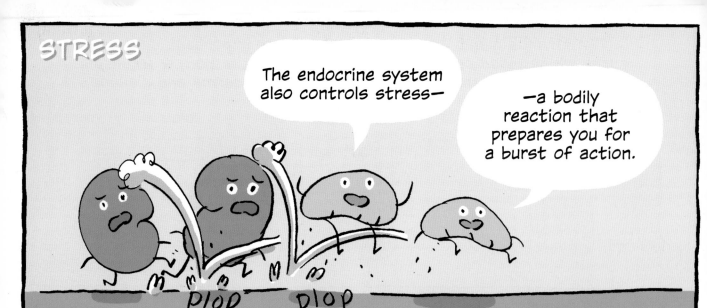

The endocrine system also controls stress—

—a bodily reaction that prepares you for a burst of action.

plop plop

Hormones like adrenalin are produced in the adrenal glands and help your body deal with stressful situations.

Next time you are in a stressful situation...

...check your heart rate. When you feel stressed, your heart races.

Your hands may get cold and sweaty.

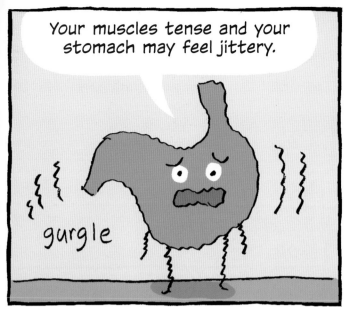

Your muscles tense and your stomach may feel jittery.

gurgle

This is because hormones are being released by your adrenal glands.

That's right!

Adrenalin prepares your body to either fight...

RAWR!

...or flee!

Mommy! *Mommy!*

zip

zip

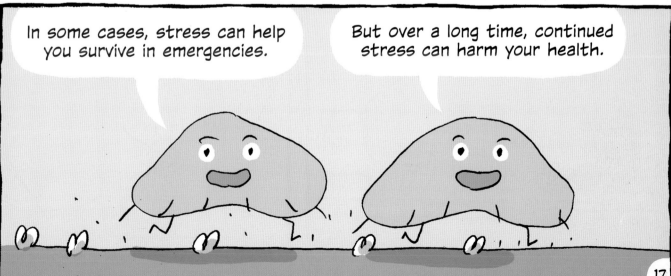

In some cases, stress can help you survive in emergencies.

But over a long time, continued stress can harm your health.

LIFE CYCLES

Humans cycle from being asleep to waking up...

...working...

...playing...

...eating, and going to the bathroom.

Another cycle is bigger than just today — your life cycle!

Like most living things, human males and females are rather different.

A lot of these differences have to do with their reproductive systems!

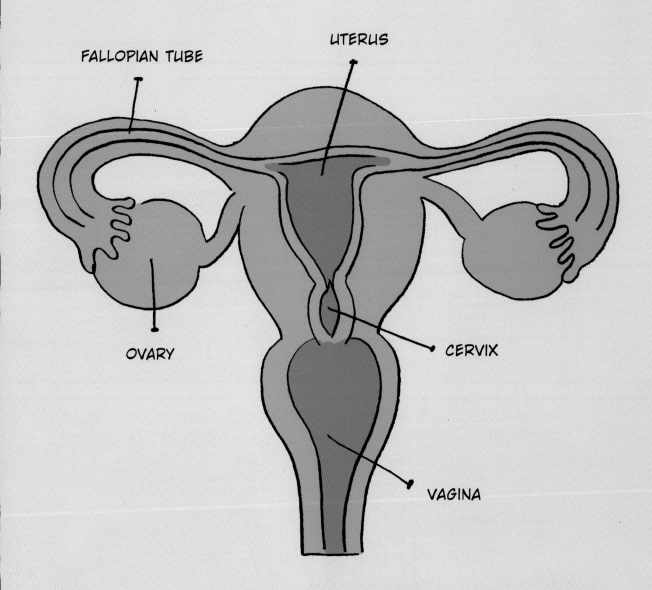

FALLOPIAN TUBE

UTERUS

OVARY

CERVIX

VAGINA

FEMALE REPRODUCTIVE SYSTEM

These systems of organs make reproduction possible.

Reproduction is the process by which animals create their own kind.

It's how you were made!

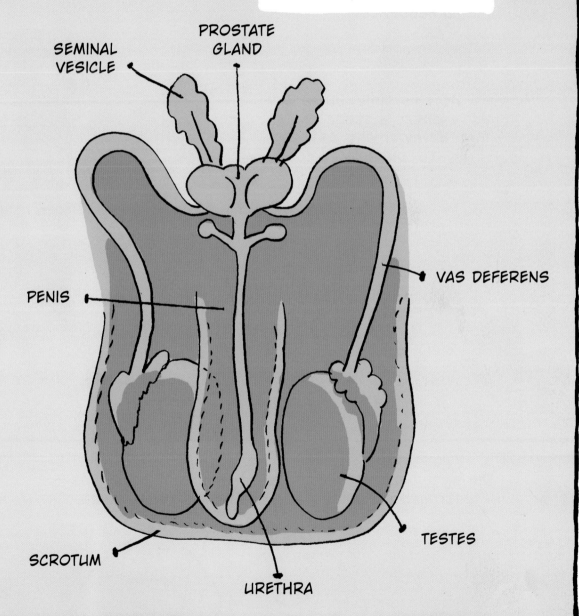

SEMINAL VESICLE

PROSTATE GLAND

VAS DEFERENS

PENIS

TESTES

SCROTUM

URETHRA

MALE REPRODUCTIVE SYSTEM

Although human beings are born with the organs necessary to reproduce, reproduction cannot occur until those organs mature.

The transition to adulthood is called **adolescence.**

At this time, humans enter a stage of development called **puberty.**

During puberty, the body is flooded with hormones—estrogen in females and testosterone in males.

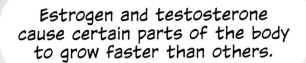

Estrogen and testosterone cause certain parts of the body to grow faster than others.

They can also cause emotions to zoom from high to low, happy to sad...

...and everything in between!

And, starting at puberty, females begin producing eggs as part of a monthly process called the **menstrual cycle**.

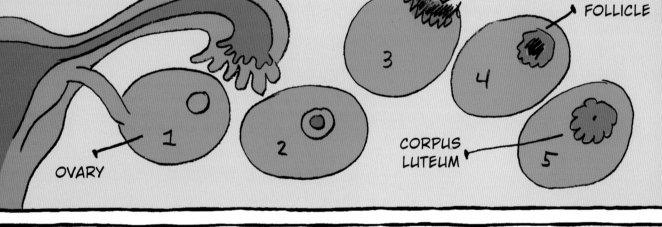

EGG NUCLEUS

FOLLICLE

OVARY

CORPUS LUTEUM

1   2   3   4   5

Inside males, **sperm** cells develop tails called flagella.

HEAD

NUCLEUS

AEROSOME

MIDPIECE

FLAGELLUM

1   2   3   4   5   6

REPRODUCTION

Fertilization occurs when sperm cells from the male are transferred to an egg cell inside the female.

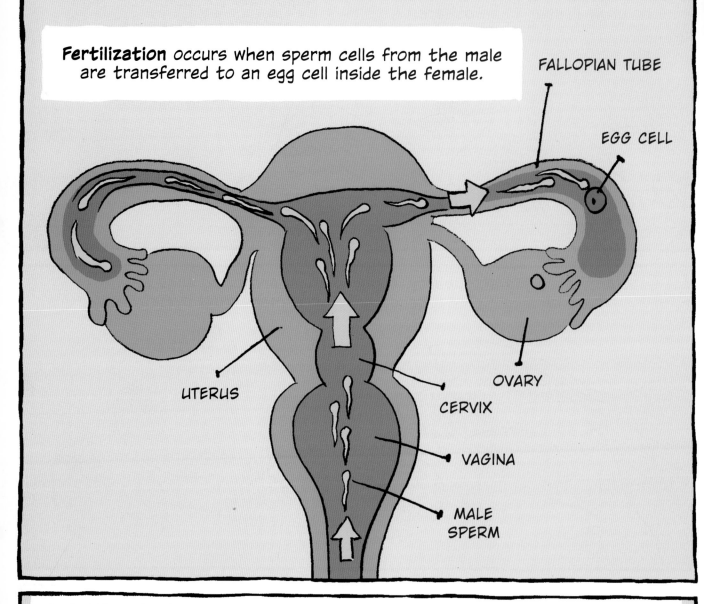

FALLOPIAN TUBE

EGG CELL

UTERUS

CERVIX

OVARY

VAGINA

MALE SPERM

And although there are millions of sperm cells, only one fertilizes the egg.

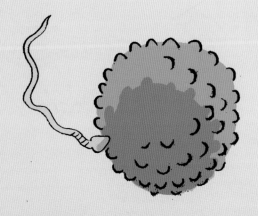

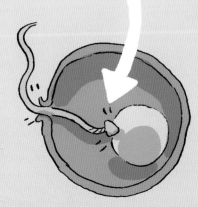

Once the egg is fertilized, it attaches to the wall of the **uterus**...

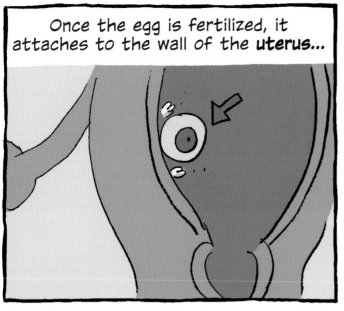

...where the cell continues a complex process of division until it becomes an **embryo.**

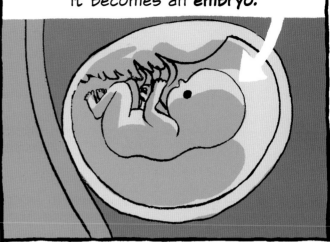

After about nine months, the cell has grown into a baby human, ready to be born!

WAH!

The process of birth is called labor.

GROWTH

After birth, humans continue to grow for many years—thanks to the endocrine system!

Humans record their growth as stages of development.

A specific hormone regulates growth in humans—

—the human growth hormone!

This hormone is made
by the pituitary gland.

It tells your
bones and muscles how
and when to grow.

All the material that makes up you came from your parents and the generations before them.

You are adding to this line with your own choices and personal experiences.

And some day, thanks to your endocrine and reproductive systems, you might even pass off that same opportunity...

...and illustrate the next generation.

GLOSSARY

adolescence a period of development between childhood and adulthood.

adrenal gland one of two glands that releases many hormones, some of which are essential to life.

cell the basic unit of all living things.

digestive system the group of organs that breaks down and absorbs food in the body.

embryo a human in the early stages of its development.

endocrine system the group of organs that produces hormones.

fertilization the joining of a male sperm cell and a female egg cell.

gland an organ that produces hormones or other substances.

hormone a chemical produced by glands that affects body functions.

hypothalamus a small area in the brain that regulates the body's level of activity.

insulin a hormone that regulates the body's use of sugars and other nutrients.

lobe a rounded part.

menstrual cycle the loss of uterine cells that occurs about once a month in most women.

nutrient a food substance that helps body growth.

organ two or more tissues that work together to do a certain job.

organ system two or more organs that do a common task.

ovaries a pair of female sex organs that stores and releases eggs.

pancreas a gland near the stomach that helps digestion.

parathyroid gland one of four glands that controls calcium levels in the body.

pineal gland a tiny gland found in the brain of human beings.

pituitary gland a gland that controls a wide range of body functions.

puberty the physical and biological changes to the body that occur during adolescence.

reproductive system the system of organs that allows human beings to create more of their own kind.

sperm the reproductive cell produced by males.

testes male sex organs that produce sperm and release the hormone testosterone.

thymus a gland that helps the body fight sickness.

thyroid a gland that controls the rate at which cells use oxygen and nutrients.

tissue a group of similar cells that do a certain job.

uterus a muscular female organ where an unborn baby develops.

FIND OUT MORE

Books

Endocrine System
by Lorrie Klosterman
(Marshall Cavendish Children's Books, 2008)

Human Body
by Richard Walker
(DK Children, 2009)

Human Body Factory: The Nuts and Bolts of Your Insides
by Dan Green
(Kingfisher, 2012)

Learning About the Endocrine and Reproductive Systems
by Melissa L. Kim
(Enslow, 2013)

Start Exploring: Gray's Anatomy: A Fact-Filled Coloring Book
by Freddy Stark
(Running Press Kids, 2011)

The Exciting Endocrine System: How Do My Glands Work?
by John Burstein
(Crabtree, 2009)

The Reproductive System
by Kerri O'Donnell
(Rosen, 2001)

The Way We Work
by David Macaulay
(Houghton Mifflin/Walter Lorraine Books, 2008)

Websites

Biology 4 Kids: Endocrine System
http://www.biology4kids.com/files/systems_endocrine.html
Get an in-depth education on all of the parts that make up the endocrine system.

E-Learning for Kids: The Endocrine System
http://www.e-learningforkids.org/health/lesson/endocrine-system/
Take a peek inside your endocrine system in this clickable lesson with bonus comprehension exercises.

Kids Biology: Endocrine System
http://www.kidsbiology.com/human_biology/endocrine-system.php
Learn all about the endocrine system by watching a short video and reading fact-filled articles complete with images of the body's organs.

Kids Health: How the Body Works
http://kidshealth.org/kid/htbw/
Select a body part to watch a video, play a word find, or read an article to learn more about its function in the human body.

National Geographic: Human Body 101 Video
http://video.nationalgeographic.com/video/101-videos/human-body-sci?source=relatedvideo
Watch an educational video that presents, discusses, and reviews the complexities of the human body.

NeoK12: Reproductive System
http://www.neok12.com/Reproductive-System.htm
Watch videos that illustrate the reproductive system, and then take grade-specific quizzes to test your knowledge.

Science Kids: Human Body for Kids
http://www.sciencekids.co.nz/humanbody.html
Sample a range of educational games, challenging experiments, and mind-bending quizzes all while learning about human body topics.

INDEX